No Backbone!
The World of Invertebrates

Crawling Crabs

by Natalie Lunis

Consultant: Bill Murphy
Marine Biologist, Northern Waters Gallery
New England Aquarium
Boston, MA

BEARPORT
PUBLISHING

NEW YORK, NEW YORK

Credits

Cover and TOC, © Mariko Yuki/Shutterstock; © EcoPrint/Shutterstock, and © Troy E. Parker/istockphoto.com; Title Page, © EcoPrint/Shutterstock; 4–5, © Ken Usami/Photodisc Green/Getty Images; 6, © Espen Rekdal/SeaPics.com; 7, © EcoPrint/Shutterstock; 8, © Michael Nichols/National Geographic/Getty Images; 9, © Espen Rekdal/SeaPics.com; 11, © John Lewis/Ecoscene; 12T, © Johann Schumacher Design; 12B, © Fred Bavendam/Minden Pictures; 13, © Gerry Ellis/Minden Pictures; 14, © Martin Harvey/Corbis; 15, © Reinhard Dirscherl/Alamy; 16, © Reinhard Dirscherl/SeaPics.com; 17, © Marilyn Kazmers/Peter Arnold, Inc.; 18, © Jeff Greenberg/Alamy; 19, © Tony Florio/Photo Researchers, Inc.; 20, © Fred Whitehead/Animals Animals Earth Scenes; 21, © Doug Perrine/SeaPics.com; 22TL, © Chris Newbert/Minden Pictures; 22TR, © Maximilian Weinzierl/Alamy; 22BL, © Brandon D. Cole/Corbis; 22BR, © Saul Gonor/SeaPics.com; 22 Spot, © Artem Mazunov/Shutterstock; 23TL, © Jim Wehtje/Photodisc Green/Getty Images; 23TR, © Bill Harrigan/SeaPics.com; 23BL, © Espen Rekdal/SeaPics.com; 23BR, © Sebastian Kaulitzki/Shutterstock.

Publisher: Kenn Goin
Editorial Director: Adam Siegel
Creative Director: Spencer Brinker
Design: Dawn Beard Creative
Photo Researcher: Amy Dunleavy

Library of Congress Cataloging-in-Publication Data

Lunis, Natalie.
  Crawling crabs / by Natalie Lunis.
      p. cm. — (No backbone! : the world of invertebrates)
  Includes bibliographical references and index.
  ISBN-13: 978-1-59716-509-9 (lib. bdg.)
  ISBN-10: 1-59716-509-3 (lib. bdg.)
  1. Crabs—Juvenile literature. I. Title.

QL444.M33L86 2008
595.3'86—dc22

2007006932

For more information, write to Bearport Publishing Company, Inc., 101 Fifth Avenue, Suite 6R, New York, New York 10003. Printed in the United States of America.

10 9 8 7 6 5 4 3 2

Contents

Spiders of the Sea

Crabs are animals with ten legs and a hard shell.

The shell is really a skeleton on the outside of a crab's body.

Insects and spiders also have skeletons on the outside of their bodies.

In fact, some people call crabs the "spiders of the sea."

Animals that have skeletons inside their bodies—such as birds, fish, and humans—have **backbones**. Animals that have skeletons on the outside of their bodies have no backbones.

Claws

There are about 4,500 kinds of crabs.

All crabs have **claws** on their two front legs.

Some kinds of crabs have one claw that is much bigger than the other.

Most kinds of crabs live in the ocean or on beaches. A few kinds live on land.

claws

Looking All Around

Crabs have eyes that are set on **eyestalks**.

The eyestalks move in different directions.

The crabs can see all around.

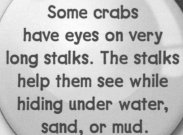

Some crabs have eyes on very long stalks. The stalks help them see while hiding under water, sand, or mud.

8

eyestalks

Grabbing a Meal

Crabs are not picky eaters.

Many eat bits of dead plants and animals.

Other crabs are hunters.

They use their strong, sharp claws to grab fish, shrimp, and worms.

Then they tear the animals apart and bring the pieces to their mouths.

Some crabs can use their claws to crack open the hard shells of clams and snails.

Surrounded by Enemies

Crabs have many enemies.

Seagulls, sea otters, and **octopuses** are just a few of the animals that eat them.

People catch and eat crabs, too.

Some crabs hunt and eat other crabs.

seagull

crab

octopus

Great Escapes

Often crabs are able to get away from their enemies.

Many crabs are good swimmers.

Their back legs are shaped like paddles.

Others can walk and even run very quickly.

Crabs usually walk and run sideways. Moving this way keeps them from tripping over their own legs!

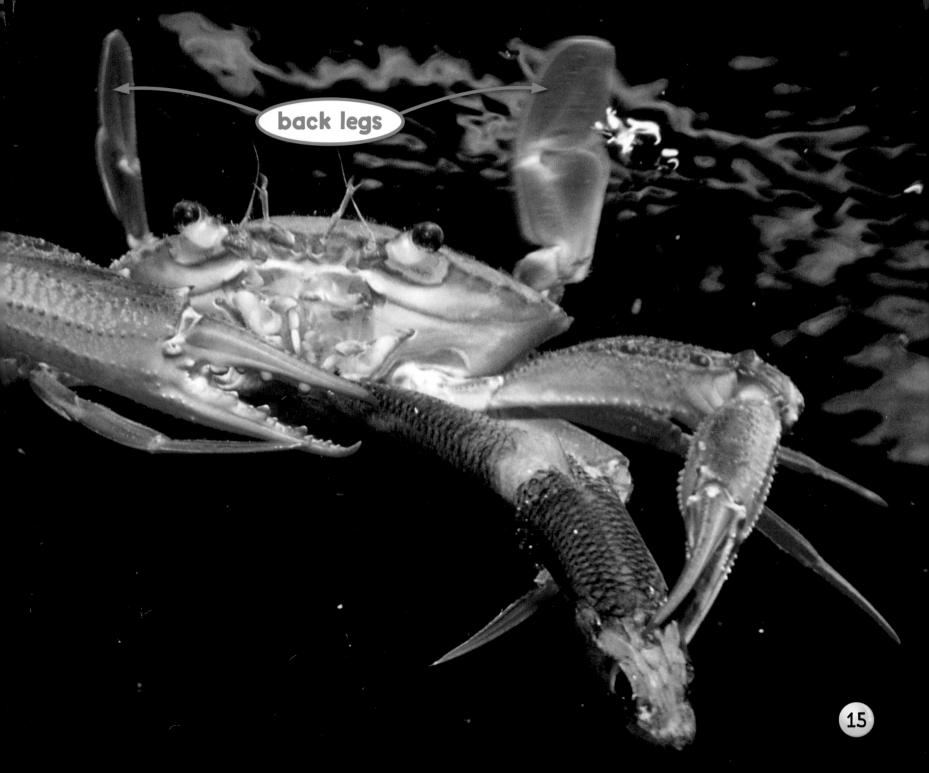

back legs

Fighting Back

Sometimes crabs fight back.

They wave their claws to try to scare an enemy away.

If the enemy doesn't back off, they give it a hard pinch.

A crab often loses a claw or leg in a fight. In time, the claw or leg grows back.

Outgrowing a Shell

A crab's hard shell protects the soft parts of its body.

The shell does not grow or stretch, however.

When a crab gets bigger, it must climb out of its shell.

This change is called molting.

empty shell

When a crab molts, a crack forms along the shell. Then the crab backs out.

old shell

crab

19

A Brand-New Shell

Crabs grow new shells under their old ones.

At first, the new shell is soft.

The crab must hide to stay safe.

After a few days, the new shell grows hard.

The crab comes out of hiding, ready to face the world again!

soft shell

Most crabs molt six or seven times during their first year of life. Then they molt once or twice a year.

A World of Invertebrates

Animals that have backbones are known as *vertebrates* (VUR-tuh-brits). Mammals, birds, fish, reptiles, and amphibians are all vertebrates.

Animals that don't have backbones are *invertebrates* (in-VUR-tuh-brits). Worms, jellyfish, snails, and crabs are all invertebrates. So are all insects and spiders. More than 95 percent of all kinds of animals are invertebrates.

Here are four invertebrates that are closely related to crabs. Like crabs, they all live in the ocean.

Lobster

Crayfish

Shrimp

Barnacles

Glossary

backbones
(BAK-*bohnz*)
a group of
connected bones
that run along
the backs of some
animals, such as
dogs, cats, and fish;
also called spines

claws
(KLAWZ) the
hand-like body
parts at the
ends of a crab's
two front legs

eyestalks
(EYE-stawks)
the stick-like body
parts that connect
a crab's eyes to its
body

octopuses
(OK-tuh-*puhss*-iz)
sea animals that
have eight arms
and a soft body

Index

Read More

Douglas, Lloyd G. *Crab*. New York: Children's Press (2005).

Herriges, Ann. *Crabs*. Minneapolis, MN: Bellwether Media (2006).

Rhodes, Mary Jo, and David Hall. *Crabs*. New York: Children's Press (2007).

Learn More Online

To learn more about crabs, visit **www.bearportpublishing.com/NoBackbone**